Think Positive!
Feel Good Images

Adult Coloring Book

Hang In There

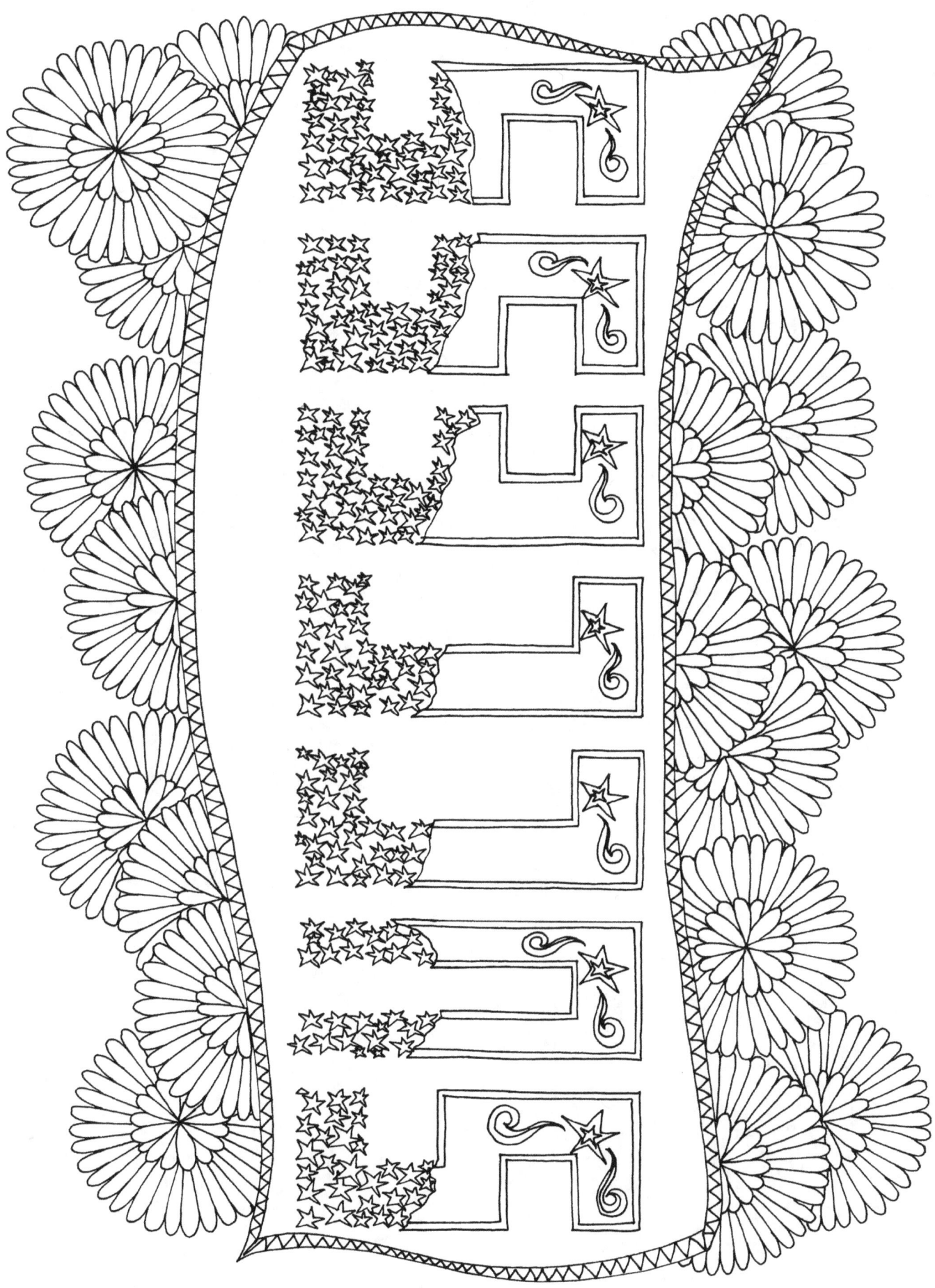

CREATIVITY

HOME IS
where
the HEART is

Acknowledgements

This book wouldn't have been possible without the beautiful images provided by artist Surabhi Kuthiala. Thanks so much for your hard work!

And much gratitude to the amazing colorist who put her own artistic spin on Surabhi's work, Patty Ann Lin, who colored the cover image. You did a beautiful job, and we couldn't be more excited to feature it.

We also need to thank all the colorists who finaled in our coloring contest: Leah Dean, Sandra Van Oevelen, Julie Bouve, Heather Haynes, Deidra Acosta, Kathy Rock, Carrie Bradley Stewart, Bianca Christina Helstrup, Deb Rucinski and Jennifer Tang. We had such a hard time picking and we loved your work!

Special mention to the colorists whose images are featured on the back of the book, Zedz Mudlong and Deb Ford. Simply gorgeous!

www.ingramcontent.com/pod-product-compliance
Lightning Source LLC
Chambersburg PA
CBHW081412280526
45788CB00009B/3075